KATARINA
WITT

by
Wayne Coffey

BLACKBIRCH PRESS, INC.

Woodbridge, Connecticut

Published by Blackbirch Press, Inc.
One Bradley Road
Woodbridge, CT 06525

©1992 Blackbirch Press, Inc.
First Edition

Manufactured in the United States of America

Editor: Bruce Glassman
Photo Research: Grace How
Illustration: Mike Eagle

Library of Congress Cataloging-in-Publication Data

Coffey, Wayne R.
    Katarina Witt / Wayne Coffey. — 1st ed.
    (Olympic Gold)
    Includes bibliographical references and index.
    Summary: A biography of the German ice skater who won the figure skating gold medal in two successive Olympic competitions.
    ISBN 1-56711-001-0
    1.Witt,Katarina,1965-   —Juvenile Literature.
2. Skaters.—Germany—Biography—Juvenile literature.
[1. Witt, Katarina, 1965-   . 2. Ice skaters.] I. Title. II.Series.
GV850.W58 C64 1992
796.91 '092—dc20
[B]
                                                           92-4699
                                                           CIP
                                                           AC

Contents

1

Beauty on Ice

"It's a fantastic feeling at the end, when the spectators get up and applaud."

Katarina Witt was standing in a very familiar spot—the victory platform. She had a bouquet of roses in her arms and a gold medal dangling from her neck.

This was the scene at the 1988 Winter Olympics, in the western Canadian city of Calgary. Witt had just finished outskating her rivals Debi Thomas of the United States, and the local favorite, Canadian Elizabeth Manley. By beating them, Witt had guaranteed her place in Olympic history. She had become the first woman in 50 years, since the era of skating legend Sonja Henie, to capture gold medals in two consecutive Olympics.

Opposite:
Katarina waves to the crowd after receiving her second consecutive gold medal in 1988.

The overflow crowd was standing and clapping. Cheers were ringing through the huge arena. The 22-year-old East German heroine was glowing. She was wearing a snug, sparkly red skating outfit. She was smiling and waving back to the crowd, a perfect picture of the "thrill of victory."

"It's a fantastic feeling at the end, when the spectators get up and applaud," Katarina said with excitement. "This fulfills your dreams. It's why you trained so hard and went through all of this."

The End of a Brilliant Career

Fulfilling dreams is something Katarina Witt knows a lot about. Those 1988 Games marked the end of her competitive skating career. By then, she had become not only one of the world's most gifted athletes, but also one of its most glamorous. Aside from the two Olympic golds, she won four world championships and six European championships. In the 1980s, the international world of women's figure skating was almost always centered on Katarina Witt.

But Katarina did more than just win. She dazzled. She wowed. She had a gift for knocking out judges and melting hearts. She combined the superior skills of an athlete with the grace of a ballerina. She had the presence of an actress and the beauty of a cover girl. The combination proved to be mostly unbeatable.

Every time Witt stepped onto the ice, the audience could feel her commanding center stage. Sometimes, you could feel it even when she wasn't on the ice. One day, when she had a little time away from the rink in Calgary, she went to a nearby mall. Her mission was to find a cowboy hat. A mass of photographers was right behind her. The cameras whirred and clicked, each aiming to get the best shot of the ice queen at the hat store. Even going for an ice cream cone turned into a media event!

Katarina Witt was the first woman in 50 years to capture gold medals in two consecutive Olympics.

In the Spotlight

When Katarina arrived at the Games, about 400 journalists from all over the globe were on hand for her press conference. There was a flurry of inquiries about her practice sessions and her views on Debi Thomas and the other top competitors. Others asked about the skating routines she was planning. Then one journalist squeezed in a different line of questioning.

"Will you marry me?" the man asked. The place erupted in laughter. Witt smiled and looked at the man, whom she had never seen before.

"We'd have to get to know each other better," she replied.

Katarina has received an estimated 40,000 letters from her admirers. Many of them have come from boys in the United States. More than a few of them were marriage proposals. A major American cosmetics company had another proposal for her: a $1 million offer to become the company's official spokeswoman.

Some high-profile athletes have difficulty handling life in the spotlight. They don't like all the questions and photographs. They dream of being an average person, who can go buy a hat without hundreds of people making a major fuss.

Katarina doesn't mind fame at all, though. And she isn't afraid to admit it. "I like to be famous and have all the people around, watching me," she said.

She doesn't mind when people talk about her looks, either. There are a number of female athletes who object when they hear people talking about how attractive they are. These women believe that such comments make people overlook their athletic skills. After all, they have worked just as hard on their skills as any of the male competitors.

Katarina is flattered when people comment on her physical appearance. She has often heard herself being compared to actress Brooke Shields, with her chestnut hair and creamy skin. "What's wrong with being compared to Brooke Shields?" Katarina wondered.

Enjoying Her Good Looks

The stir surrounding Katarina has not always pleased her rivals. She has been criticized for being a flirt. Before one Olympic practice, Witt slowly peeled off her warmup pants, in a make-believe striptease. Underneath she was wearing purple tights. Another time, in a top competition, Katarina skated as a belly dancer.

Some people have accused Katarina of "playing up" to the judges with her sexy looks and movements. Opposing coaches have been known to make cracks about her skimpy skating costumes. Some of them claim that her beauty makes judges inflate her scores, even when she hasn't skated her best.

"I like to be famous and have all the people around, watching me," Katarina said.

But to Katarina, skating is a sport that is full of theatre and visual appeal. And eye-catching costumes are a way to enhance one's appeal. "It's an expression of grace and beauty," she once said. "I think every man prefers a well-shaped women rather than someone built in the shape of a ball.

9

Katarina allows the excitement of the crowd to boost her performance. The crowd, in turn, always enjoys her dramatic flair for skating.

When I wear the right costume, I feel much better. Why shouldn't we stress what we have that is attractive?"

Katarina has used her beauty as part of her art form. She has become perhaps the most celebrated figure skater in history. She is definitely the most photographed.

The Thrill of an Audience

Throughout her career, Katarina has been inspired by crowds. She would get a rush of adrenaline whenever she'd sense the audience respond to her skating. It often seemed that the more important the competition and the more attention she got, the greater would be her performance.

In sports, this is known as "coming through in the clutch." It is a quality that only true champions have. Katarina had a lot of it, and she has the medals to prove it. You don't get to the Olympic victory platform by being just another pretty face.

To Katarina, skating is a sport that is full of theatre and visual appeal.

2

A Love for Skating

"I remember thinking, 'This is for me.'"

Katarina Witt (pronounced *Vitt*) was born in December, 1965, in Karl-Marx-Stadt. That area is an industrial city in the Saxony region of what was then East Germany. Her father, Manfred Witt, worked as a director of an agricultural center, where various crops were raised. Kathe Witt, Katarina's mom, worked as a physical therapist.

When Katarina was five years old, she and her mother would walk by a skating rink every day on the way to kindergarten. The rink was called the Kuchwald Ice Arena. Little Katarina became enchanted by the swift and graceful movements of the skaters. She kept asking her mother if she could give the sport a try. One day, Kathe Witt agreed.

First Time on the Ice

A trainer laced up her skates. The ice was wet around the sides of the rink, where the ice-surfacing machine had just passed by. Kathe Witt told her daughter to move toward the center. "I was wearing my street clothes," Katarina said. "My mommy told me to go into the middle or otherwise my panty hose would get wet."

Katarina first put on skates at the age of five.

Unsure at first, the girl skated slowly away from the sides. The air in the rink was cold and crisp. Gradually, she became more comfortable. She discovered she liked the feeling of gliding over the ice. "I remember thinking, 'This is for me,'" Katarina recalled later.

"She took to the ice like a duck to water," said Bernd Egert, the head coach of the Karl-Marx-Stadt sports club. "She obviously was a natural from the first time she put on skates."

The little girl was very happy about learning to skate. But her parents were not so sure. They preferred that she learn to dance. Katarina gave dancing a try, but it simply wasn't as exciting as being out on the ice for her. She learned to do the polka, and then pleaded with her parents to let her go back to the rink.

Improving a Natural Gift

Manfred and Kathe Witt went along with their daughter's wishes. Before long, Katarina joined a skating class. The lessons had already started when she began. The instructor told her she would have to catch up, learning a year's worth of instruction in only six months. Katarina did just that. It was clear that she was the most gifted pupil in the class.

Recognizing the young girl's natural ability, Egert recruited her for a special training
program. She became part of
East Germany's well-known
sports system, in which young
children who were judged to
have Olympic potential were
placed in a fast-track group.

> *"She took to the ice like a duck to water," said Coach Bernd Egert. "She obviously was a natural from the first time she put on skates."*

After undergoing thorough tests, these
youngsters' lives were changed completely.
They were put on rigid schedules and spent
long hours practicing. Often they saw more
of their coaches than they did of their
families. There was very little time allowed
for seeing friends or playing games.

For years, East Germany was widely
criticized for its approach to sports. Many
people believed it was not healthy for
children to be pulled away from their
families at such a young age. The critics
said such an approach made it very hard for
these youngsters to become well-adjusted,
well-rounded people.

But at the time, East German authorities
were more concerned with the bottom line.
The Olympics were extremely important to
government leaders. In the Olympics in the
1970s and 1980s, only the Soviet Union
captured more gold medals than East Germany. To East German leaders, this was
proof that they were doing things right.

Change to the East German System

Gold medals or not, the sports system did not survive the great political changes that swept through Germany in the late 1980s. Germany had been divided into East and West Germany ever since World War II. But the two countries united in the fall of 1990. The strict Communist society of East Germany became a thing of the past. East Germans were given more freedom. Their government no longer dictated how much people would earn or where they would work. Citizens made their own choices and could live their lives as they wanted—and this was true in sports as well.

As a young girl, Katarina had no complaints with the system. She loved to skate, and she was getting plenty of opportunity to do it. Her progress was quick. She showed enormous flexibility and grace. Even as a child, she had a rare gift for fighting off nervousness and concentrating only on her skating. This quality would become a special Katarina Witt trademark throughout her career.

Help from a New Coach

At age nine, Katarina caught the eye of Jutta Mueller, a serious, round woman who was known as one of the world's top figure-

skating coaches. Mueller's skaters have won more than 50 international medals. Only the most outstanding young talents were given a chance to work with her. Mueller is known for her strict, hard-driving ways. One of her most famous pupils—before Katarina—was Anett Pötzsch. She captured the 1980 Olympic gold medal in Lake Placid. Anett Pötzsch is no stranger to Katarina—she's married to Axel Witt, Katarina's older brother.

Coach Jutta Mueller was strict and demanding. Even a broken leg did not stop her from supervising all of Katarina's practices.

As expected, coach Mueller pushed Katarina hard. The young skater left home in the morning and often wouldn't get back

Even as a child, Katarina had a rare gift for fighting off nervousness and concentrating only on her skating.

home until after dinner. The coach wanted constant, intense practice. She would leave nothing at all to chance. Later in Katarina's career, "Frau Mueller," as she was known, spent hours fine-tuning every detail of Katarina's routines. She worked on everything from her makeup to her hairstyle, and the way Katarina would project herself to her audience. It was Frau Mueller who taught Katarina to pick out one man's face during a performance. The coach told Katarina to make constant eye contact with that man. The technique helped to heighten Katarina's connection with the crowd.

Jutta Mueller was as demanding of herself as she was of Katarina. At one point, the coach suffered a broken leg in an accident. To Mueller, this was no reason to miss practice. She instructed the ambulance driver to take her to the rink where she supervised Katarina's workout from a stretcher.

A Demanding Coach

The coach's entire life was about teaching figure skating. She was a maker of champions. Nothing was more important than that. "When I start to train children, they are not stars at the beginning," Frau Mueller said. "They are talented athletes. I could see Katarina had promise. Of course, there was a lot of work to be done."

Skating for a perfectionist like Frau Mueller was far from easy. There were times when young Katarina would get angry or frustrated by her coach's harsh ways. Sometimes, Katarina would feel like screaming out, "Why don't you get off my back?" Such feelings were very understandable. Still, Katarina knew there were no shortcuts to success. If she wanted to be a champion someday, she had to invest the time and effort to get there.

Katarina knew there were no shortcuts to success. If she wanted to be a champion someday, she had to invest the time and the effort to get there.

Katarina stayed with it. She listened to her coach and dedicated herself to her sport. By the time she began her teens, Katarina Witt's name was becoming known well beyond the town of Karl-Marx-Stadt. Already, the investment was paying off.

3

Golden Olympian

"That girl is amazing."

One of the hardest feats in figure skating is a triple jump. It involves leaping off the ice and doing three full turns before landing. Katarina Witt did her first triple jump at age 11. Even Jutta Mueller had to be a little bit pleased about that. She had a young skater with great natural ability just waiting to be molded into a champion.

Katarina had plenty of other moves, as well. By the time she was 14, she was tenth in the world championships. One year later, she moved up to fifth. In 1982, at the age of 17, she skated to her first European championship, and finished second overall in the world.

Opposite:
By the time Katarina was 15 years old, she ranked fifth in the world championships. By age 17, she had won a European championship and finished second in the world.

International Stardom

Katarina was just getting warmed up. The 1984 Olympics were held in Sarajevo, Yugoslavia, and it was there that 18-year-old Katarina Witt skated into international stardom. In the biggest competition of her life, Katarina performed as freely as if she were just out for a Sunday skate in the park. She completed perfect, elegant pirouettes (turns). Her triple jumps were incredible. And her radiance and charm came through in full force.

Katarina Witt and American Rosalyn Sumners became the leaders as the event neared completion. Only a fraction of a point separated the two skaters as they entered into the final long-skating program. Whirling, flowing, and jumping over the ice, Katarina put on a dazzling display. Rosalyn Sumners matched her almost move for move. When it was all over and the judges' scores had been tallied, Katarina Witt was awarded the gold medal.

By the age of 18, Katarina had won her first gold medal at the 1984 Olympics in Sarajevo, Yugoslavia.

The 1984 Olympic victory marked the beginning of Katarina Witt's dominance in the world of women's figure skating. Later that year, she captured the European and world titles. She repeated the same feat a year later. In the 1985 world competition, held in Tokyo, Japan, Katarina was the only non-Soviet skater to place first in any division. Skating to the music of American composer George Gershwin, Katarina delivered a stunning freestyle program. She astounded the crowd with four flawless triple jumps. She glided over the ice with poise and grace. One observer termed it "a golden performance, a hard—perhaps impossible—act to follow."

Katarina had a burning desire to win, every time she competed.

Stare Down in Tokyo

The only competitor with a chance to surpass Katarina that night was American Tiffany Chin. Tiffany skated after her East German rival. Rather than retiring to the locker room, Katarina stayed at the rail of the rink. Her gaze was fixed on Tiffany—and there were many people who complained long and loud about it later.

One of the sport's long-established courtesies is that you never watch another skater perform. It is considered to be in "bad taste"—like talking while a tennis player is serving.

Katarina's actions seemed to be a clear attempt to pressure Tiffany. It was the same as saying, "Go ahead, let's see what you can do." She was widely criticized for her bad manners, especially after Tiffany didn't produce her best effort.

Katarina had a burning desire to win, every time she competed. Her drive to succeed was often underestimated, perhaps because of her beauty. She may have taken the desire too far with Tiffany. Even for top athletes, competition can go too far. And poor sportsmanship is not acceptable behavior, no matter what the circumstances are. But there was no question about Katarina's single-minded will to be the top figure skater in the world.

A New Rival

Between 1984 and 1988, the only occasion when Katarina didn't hold the title was in 1986. That was when Debi Thomas upset her in the world championships, with a magnificent display in Geneva, Switzerland. Debi was Katarina's archrival through most of the 1980s. It was almost impossible to talk about one without mentioning the other. Blessed with extraordinary athletic ability, Debi was known for her soaring jumps and daring routines.

A year later, Debi and Katarina were back for another duel on the ice. The 1987 world meet was staged in Cincinnati, Ohio. The competition, as always, was graded in three different areas: compulsories (required moves and steps), the short program, and the long, or freestyle, program.

Opposite:
Debi Thomas was a long-time rival of Katarina's. Known for her dramatic jumps and routines, Debi was the only skater capable of stealing the spotlight from Katarina.

25

In the compulsories, skaters perform a series of basic moves, such as Figure 8's, jumps and turns, to show their command of the sport's fundamentals. There is more room for individual creativity in the short program—and even more in the long program, which accounts for 50 percent of the skater's final score.

Both women had their troubles at first. Debi's short program was not her best effort, and Katarina's compulsories were dull. For the East German star, this was a career-long pattern. She loved the artistry and freedom of freestyle skating. And she devoted most of her energy and concentration to that part of the competition. To Katarina, the compulsories were like a pesky mosquito—an annoyance that wouldn't go away.

"I absolutely despise them," she once said of the compulsories.

Debi's Incredible Performance

Defending her hard-earned title, Debi came out for her long program. She then completed what many believe was the greatest performance of her career. The Californian (who was the first black skater to win a world title) produced five breathtaking triple jumps. She had the pro-American crowd in a frenzy, with her soaring moves and total command. A second consecutive title seemed almost guaranted.

> *"When I go out on the ice, I just think about my skating," Katarina said. "There are many people watching . . . . I skate for them."*

Katarina Witt was up next. She had almost no margin for error. Unless she somehow found a way to outdo Debi Thomas, her standing as the queen of the rink would be a thing of the past. That honor would now belong to Debi Thomas.

It was probably the most pressure Katarina Witt ever faced before a performance. She dealt with it by trying to close her mind to the competition. Sure, she was nervous when she went out on the ice. She tried not to think about what she had to do to win. She tried to forget how many points she had to pile up and what moves she had to perform to get those points. Instead, Katarina forced herself to focus on her skating. By concentrating on the challenge itself, she found she could deliver better results.

"When I go out on the ice, I just think about my skating," she said. "I forget it is a competition. There are many people watching on television, and many spectators. I skate for them. You can feel whether they like it."

A Special Effort

There was no question that the crowd was impressed that day in Cincinnati. Katarina

Witt responded to Debi's best effort with one of her own. She, too, hit five triples. She executed two double axels (twirling jumps), another very difficult move. Every flowing spin, every moment, was filled with artistry. Katarina received top scores from seven of the nine judges. Against great odds, she had recaptured the world title. Afterward, she said great preparation went into her effort. Katarina Witt did not like the idea of being second for another year.

"I trained harder than I ever have," she said. "It wasn't easy to skate after Debi, but myself, I had a good feeling. I said to myself, 'Relax, you can do it.'"

Best Again in the World

Indeed, she did do it. After her performance in Cincinnati, there wasn't any talk about judges being swayed by her flirty smiles and radiant looks. Katarina was simply a champion. Debi Thomas was among those who praised her.

"That girl is amazing," Debi said. "She's tough. She just goes out and does what she has to."

Coach Jutta Mueller was impressed, too. "She did a program I have seen a hundred times, and today it was as if I'd seen it for the first time," the coach said. "Really, at her best, nobody could come close."

4

Victories and Changes

*"It was the last time,
and I am very sad about that."*

The Katarina Witt–Debi Thomas rivalry seemed to heat up after the showdown in Cincinnati. It was more than just two tremendous skating talents. Everything about the skaters was different.

Katarina was from a Communist country; Debi was an American. Katarina's specialty was her artistry and grace, while Debi's was her unsurpassed jumping and bold, athletic routines.

Another difference was that Katarina thrived on the attention and fanfare her skating prompted. Debi always seemed most comfortable on the ice. All the questions about her battles with Katarina made

Debi ill at ease. On top of everything else, the two skaters had a "cool" personal relationship. Despite years of competing against one another, they never developed a friendship off the ice.

Olympics in Calgary, Canada

As the 1988 Olympic Games began, most of the attention was focused on the ongoing competition between the American and the East German. And the attention became greater because of an odd coincidence: both Katarina and Debi selected the opera *Carmen* for their long program.

Both women tried to downplay the idea that it was a two-woman competition. Katarina stated that Debi's fellow Americans, Caryn Kadavy and Jill Trenary, were also fine skaters who warranted watching—as did Canada's Elizabeth Manley. Debi, too, did what she could to get the press off the *Carmen* rivalry theme. Said Katarina, "Whoever has the strongest nerves here has the best chance."

A massive crowd packed the ice skating arena to see the showdown between Katarina and Debi.

The Olympic drama unfolded as promised. Debi Thomas skated superbly in the compulsories, finishing second overall. Katarina, meanwhile, was able to put aside her dislike for the event enough to place third. After both skaters performed well in the short program, the anticipated climax was at hand. All around Calgary, people were buzzing about the women's figure skating competition. A massive crowd was jammed into the arena for the final. It seemed as if most reporters in the world were on hand to witness the results. The skaters' efforts to downplay their rivalry were hopeless now. The battle for the gold had, in fact, come down to the *Carmens*.

The Carmens *Duel*

Katarina skated first. Her performance was full of her usual flair and drama. (The opera ends with Carmen dying, so Katarina did her own interpretation of that, collapsing into a dramatic fall in the center of the rink as the performance ended.)

It was a carefully choreographed routine. The question was: was it too careful?

Katarina received nearly perfect scores for artistic impression, which she almost always did. But her marks for her technical performance were average. Katarina had not attempted many daring jumps or elaborate maneuvers. She kept to the basics, and the judges made her pay for it.

Katarina's caution gave Debi Thomas the chance she needed to grab the gold. A solid showing by Debi was probably all she needed to fulfill her lifelong dream. But the

31

Katarina's *Carmen* performance at the 1988 Games earned her a gold medal.

California Carmen refused to play it safely. Debi Thomas went all the way. She was like a home-run hitter in baseball. She stepped up and swung from the heels. When you swing that hard and you make contact, the ball sails into orbit, you look great, and you get all the glory. When you don't make contact, you strike out.

(Continued on page 49)

1984

Sarajevo, Yugoslavia

STYLE AND GRACE

At the age of 18, Katarina skated to international stardom in Sarajevo, Yugoslavia. Her dazzling display of whirls, perfect pirouettes, and incredible triple jumps won her a gold medal for figure skating. Her wonderfully relaxed style and dramatic costumes also helped her to win the hearts of all who watched her perform.

THE GAMES IN YUGOSLAVIA

Left: Opening ceremonies officially began the Sarajevo Games. *Below:* American skater Tiffany Chin was an early rival of Katarina's. After the 1984 Olympics, the two skaters competed in Tokyo at the world skating championships. It was there that Katarina stood at the rail of the rink and gazed at Tiffany while she did her routine. Because of this, Katarina was criticized for showing poor sportsmanship.

THE GLORY OF THE GOLD

Katarina thanks the crowd after the 1984 competition. American silver medalist Rosalyn Sumners (in white) and Soviet bronze medalist Kira Ivanova share the spotlight.

1988

CALGARY, CANADA

THE GAMES IN CANADA

Colorful and grand opening ceremonies marked the beginning of the XV Winter Olympiad in Calgary, Canada.

Carmen Wins the Day

Katarina was a more seasoned and a more careful skater in the 1988 Olympic Games. Although she only placed third in the compulsories, she came alive for her long program. Based on the tragic opera *Carmen*, Katarina's performance captivated the arena. She received nearly perfect scores from the judges for her artistic impression.

THREE OLYMPIC CHAMPIONS

Below: American Debi Thomas—Katarina's great rival—also used *Carmen* for her long program in the 1988 competition. Although she skated brilliantly, Debi made a few major mistakes that cost her the gold. *Left:* Canadian Elizabeth Manley made an impressive showing at the 1988 Games. Her long program performance earned her a silver medal. *Opposite:* Medalists Elizabeth Manley, Katarina Witt, and Debi Thomas wave to the crowd at the 1988 awards ceremony.

AFTER THE SECOND GOLD

Above: Coach Jutta Mueller glows as Katarina shows off her gold medal. *Right:* In 1991, Katarina and American star Brian Boitano teamed up for a spectacular touring ice show that traveled throughout America and was seen by hundreds of thousands of fans.

A New Olympic Role

Katarina was asked by CBS to be a commentator during their coverage of the 1992 Winter Olympics in Albertville, France.

(Continued from page 32)

Debi Takes a Chance

Moments before Debi took to the ice, she got a last-second pep talk from her coach, Alex McGowan. The two had worked together for 11 years. It had come down to these few minutes. The coach said, "You're the best. Show them that you're the best. This is your moment. Now, do it!" They slapped hands and Debi skated out.

In the opening seconds of her routine, Debi attempted the toughest move in her routine, called the triple-toe-triple-toe. Like most skaters, Debi thrives on fan reaction. She knew that if she could nail such a spectacular move, the crowd would go berserk, and it would almost be as if all the enthusiasm was just pouring right into Debi's skates. She would be off and flying toward a gold.

Debi had performed the triple-toe move flawlessly all week in practice. Now, she built up speed, soared off the ice, and went into a tight spin. But she lost her balance slightly on her landing, coming down awkwardly on two skates, rather than on one.

It was a crushing emotional blow to Debi. Instead of hearing the crowd roar, she heard it gasp in disappointment. She took her best swing, but Debi didn't hit a home run. In fact, she didn't come close. She missed on several other jumps after that.

49

"Once I missed [on the first one], my heart wasn't in it," Debi said afterward. Her disappointment increased when Canadian Elizabeth Manley passed her to take the silver medal. Manley thrilled fellow Canadians with a superb performance that included five perfect triple jumps. Debi Thomas had to settle for the bronze medal.

The Olympic gold, for the second straight time, belonged to East Germany's wonder woman. Even if Katarina hadn't delivered her most unforgettable performance, there was no disputing that she was one of the greatest athletes in Olympic figure-skating history.

An Important Decision

Before the 1988 Olympics, Katarina had decided that she was ready to wrap up her amateur career soon. All the years of pressure and practice had taken a toll. It was time to move on. A month after the Olympics, she went to Budapest, Hungary, for the world championships. It was the final competition of Katarina's career.

"This is the last warmup I will ever do," Katarina remembered. ". . . It was hard for me."

No one was surprised when Katarina emerged on top in Budapest, too. It was her fourth world championship title. Again skating her long program to *Carmen*, she finished ahead of Elizabeth Manley and

Debi Thomas—just as she had a month before in the Olympics.

But in some ways, it was a bittersweet victory, because there would be no more to follow. She had wanted to go out with the most memorable skating of her career. She wanted to give the fans in Budapest one final way in which to remember her. But Katarina was still physically and emotionally drained from the Olympics. Her usual passion and concentration just weren't there.

"When I went out there to warm up, I thought, 'This is the last warmup I will ever do,'" she remembered. "And when I started the free skating, I thought the same, over and over. It was hard for me."

Katarina closed her amateur career in 1988 at the world championships in Budapest, Hungary.

51

Canadian Elizabeth Manley challenged both Katarina and Debi Thomas in Calgary.

No More Next Times

In previous competitions where Katarina fell short of her own expectations, she felt better knowing that she could do better next time. Suddenly, there were no more next times.

She had been competing for 13 years. She had made huge sacrifices by devoting her life to becoming a champion. And she had succeeded as few skaters ever have. But Katarina's instincts told her that it was time to start a new chapter in her life. There were so many other things she wanted to do.

Changes are hard to deal with. Skating had been Katarina's identity for as long as she could remember. The future was full of promise, but it was also unknown. It isn't easy to give up something that has brought you so much glory and gold.

Katarina waved warmly to the crowd as she skated away from her amateur career in Budapest. A short time later, she answered questions from reporters. These men and women had been tracking her career all over the world. Many of them had been there for her greatest triumphs. They had watched her rapid rise from promising teenager to gold medalist. Now the press wanted to know about her future plans, and about how Katarina felt she was going to cope with her new life.

Skating had been Katarina's identity for as long as she could remember.

A Bright Future

She spoke about the change. She explained that her gut sense told her it was time for something new. She told them about how she had practiced for hours every day, year after year. She explained that there's only so much one person can do before getting "burned out."

As she answered questions, Katarina Witt fought back her tears. She was going out a champion, the exit every athlete dreams of. But that didn't make it any easier. "It was the last time, and I am very sad about that," she said.

5

Life off the Ice

"Now I have so many possibilities.
It's all so new, so wonderful."

Katarina Witt had even more changes to deal with than she knew. Within 18 months of winning her second gold medal, East Germany no longer existed. There was only one Germany now. East German society had crumbled. And the sports system that had nurtured her career crumbled with it.

For years, Katarina had been the shining symbol of success for East Germany. The Communist leaders would point to Katarina proudly and say, "How can you criticize a system that produces an intelligent, articulate, and medal-winning talent such as Katarina Witt?"

At every opportunity Katarina voiced her support for the system. She said she wouldn't have become a champion if she had lived in another country. Even though her family wasn't wealthy, she always had access to the best coaches and facilities.

Defending the Old System

Katarina's success enabled her to live a life of luxury. She owned an expensive sports car. She had several spacious apartments to live in. She was paid over $1,000 a month. This may not seem like a lot in U.S. terms, but in East Germany, it made her a wealthy young woman. An average schoolteacher at that time was earning about $90 per month.

When fellow citizens learned of Katarina's favored treatment, some of them became angry. The guiding principle of communism is to eliminate economic classes. The idea is for everyone to be equal, with no rich and no poor. The fact that their national heroine was scooting around Berlin in a swanky sports car irritated many people.

Katarina's success enabled her to live a life of luxury.

Katarina became an almost instant outcast in her own land. She was criticized in letters to newspapers and on call-in radio and television programs. One time, she came home to find her apartment had been

burglarized. The place had been turned upside down. Jewelry and special keepsakes had been stolen.

Feelings of Betrayal

Shaken by this sudden turn, Katarina was angry and confused. She had done what her country had asked her to do all those years. She pushed herself tirelessly. She made skating her entire life. Now, after bringing glory to her homeland, she was treated as a villain.

Katarina tried to understand why people felt this way. She knew that the failing economy had stirred up many fears about what would become of the country. She also knew people were furious at party leaders as things became worse and worse. As a symbol of the way things had been in the past, Katarina was a natural target.

"I fully understand why they are critical of me," Katarina explained. "But I think people should try to understand that all over the world, athletes who do well make a lot of money and live better than the average citizen. Look at the United States. You have many, many baseball and basketball players earning over $1 million a year. That's more than your typical schoolteacher, too."

"I really , really like the United States . . . (but) East Germany is my home," *Katarina said.*

Thinking about America

Things got so bad that, for awhile, Katarina actually considered leaving her country. She has always had a special fondness for the United States. She loves wearing blue jeans and sweatshirts, listening to American rock stars, and going to dance clubs. She also realized she would be free to pursue whatever opportunities she wanted in America.

As a professional skater in the 1990s, Katarina worked with American skating star Brian Boitano.

Ultimately, though, Katarina decided not to leave Germany. "I really, really like the United States," she said. "I'd like to spend as much time as I can here. (But) East Germany is my home. You can't just leave over a dispute."

Katarina has gained almost as much success after her competitive skating career as she had during it. She has teamed with American skating star, Brian Boitano, in an incredible touring ice show. She has worked with companies to develop her own line of clothing. She has taken acting lessons, too, and has a dream to one day appear in movies.

The Changes in Germany

It is funny that the same changes that made Katarina's life so uncomfortable have actually been an advantage to her. Under the old system, she was not free to pursue money-making ventures. Decisions were made for her about what she could do. Under the old East German system, government authorities always had the final say.

Now, in a free-market economy, Katarina was busy making deals. She has gone from successful ice skater to successful businesswoman. Her career plans are based solely on her own needs and desires. Katarina had always liked the free-skating part of the

Opposite:
Katarina plans to thrill audiences with her skating in the coming years as a professional. She also dreams of one day becoming an actress.

competitions best. This new sort of freedom agrees with her, too.

"Now I have so many possibilities," she said. "It's all so new, so wonderful. People come to me and ask me what I want to do."

Her hope for the future doesn't mean Katarina doesn't miss the excitement she got from competition. She spent years sharpening her competitive drive, pushing herself to the top. These days Katarina's skating performances are not directed toward finishing first. Now, she skates purely to entertain people. There are no scorecards to watch for. There are no judges to impress.

"I still skate every day, but I skate to give a good performance, not to win a gold medal," Katarina says.

"I still skate every day, but I skate to give a good performance, not to win a gold medal," she said.

Anyone who saw her skate when she *did* win the gold medals won't forget it. Katarina has often said she wants to be remembered for starting a new era in figure skating. Her goal was to be not just an athlete, but an artist as well.

Many people agree that her mission was accomplished. Katarina brought major changes to her sport. She heightened the art of interpreting music. She had a gift for being a storyteller on skates and transforming herself into the character she portrayed.

She made an art form out of being graceful, knowing what spectators wanted, and then giving it to them. Katarina was born with those stunning good looks. But her hard work was what made her into an irresistible performer on ice.

Katarina is eager to continue her new pursuits and to take on fresh challenges. But she also knows that nothing is likely to replace figure skating in her heart. She had loved the ice the first time she ever stepped on it. Even after all the attention, after winning a pair of precious gold medals, her passion never faded.

"The role I like best is champion," she has said. She will certainly always be that.

Glossary

amateur   An athlete who does not compete for money.

axel   A twirling jump in skating that is considered one of the most difficult.

choreography   The art of creating dance routines.

communism   A system of government in which the state owns the country's means of production.

compulsories   Required moves and steps.

duel   A contest between two persons.

economy   The management of the income and spending of a government.

Frau   The German word for "Mrs."

freestyle   Performance with emphasis on original moves.

fundamentals   The basics or foundations.

pirouette   Whirling around on the point of the toe.

polka   A fast dance for couples.

rival   One who competes against another.

routine   A regular or planned performance.

For Further Reading

Arnold, Caroline. *The Olympic Summer Games*. New York: Franklin Watts, 1991.

Arnold, Caroline. *The Olympic Winter Games*. New York: Franklin Watts, 1991.

Bailey, Donna. *Skating*. Austin: Raintree Steck-Vaughn, 1991.

Buck, Roy. *Tiffany Chin: A Dream on Ice*. Chicago: Childrens Press, 1986.

Tatlow, Peter. *The Olympics*. New York: Franklin Watts, 1988.

Index

B
Berlin, Germany, 55
Boitano, Brian, 46, 57, 58
Budapest, Hungary, 50, 51

C
Calgary, Canada, 5, 7, 30, 31, 39, 40, 52
Carmen, 30, 31, 32, 42, 45, 50
Chin, Tiffany, 23, 25, 37
Cincinnati, Ohio, 25, 27, 29

E
East Germany, 12, 13, 15, 16, 50, 54, 55, 56, 58
reunification, 16, 58
sports system, 15
Egert, Bernd, 14, 15

G
Geneva, Switzerland, 25
Gershwin, George, 23

H
Henie, Sonja, 5

I
Ivanova, Kira, 38

K
Kadavy, Caryn, 30
Karl-Marx-Stadt, East Germany, 12, 19
Karl-Marx-Stadt sports club, 14

Kuchwald Ice Arena, 12, 13

M
Manley, Elizabeth, 5, 30, 45, 50, 52
McGowan, Alex, 49
Mueller, Jutta, 16–19, 21, 28, 46

O
Olympic Games, 15
1984 Winter Games, 22–23, 33–38
1988 Winter Games, 5, 6, 30–32, 39–46

P
Pötzsch, Anett, 17

S
Sarajevo, Yugoslavia, 22, 33, 34, 37
Saxony, 12
Soviet Union, 15
Sumners, Rosalyn, 22, 38

T
Thomas, Debi, 5, 7, 25–32, 45, 49–51, 52
Tokyo, Japan, 22–23, 37
Trenary, Jill, 30

W
West Germany, 16

Photo Credits

Cover: Focus on Sports
Pages 5, 10, 20, 32, 33–47, 52, 59: Focus on Sports; page
24: © Michel Pondmareff/Gamma Liaison; page 48:
© CBS/Gamma Liaison; page 57:
© Oscar Abolafia/Gamma Liaison.

DATE DUE		
FEB 0 6 1996		
SEP 18		
OCT 24		
DEC 0 6		
JAN 0 8		
JAN 2 3		

921
WIT

Coffey, Wayne R.

16402

Katarina Witt.

SWATARA JR. H.S. - CDSD

397023 01495   05306D